The Doogri Method™ Piano Curriculum

The Doogri Method™ utilizes an evidence-based piano curriculum that guarantees results. Every student regardless of ability will learn to read music notation and play the piano independently. In this second book in the series, note-reading milestones must be met before continuing with the next book in the series.

This curriculum is protected for Licensed Developmental Music Education LDME® professionals trained to teach with the Doogri Method™. This is in no way transferable license to non-accredited teachers without a contract. Any unauthorized use of this curriculum or violation of these terms are subject to sanctions.

The Doogri Institute requires all Licensed Developmental Music Education LDME® professionals to submit milestone markers for each student. Lack of submission of this data is subject to enforcement of infringement laws.

Sales and distribution outside of these parameters are not permitted. The material and terms are protected under copyright. Violators will be held responsible for all costs related to the seizure and return of unauthorized use of material(s).

Parents and Students: to inquire about your piano teacher's credentials and contractual agreement, please check with the Doogri Institute about the terms of use for this book, online at http://www.Doogri.org.

by Doogri Institute

Copyright © 2019, Doogri Institute.

Published by Doogri Institute, San Diego, CA

Composer: Henny Kupferstein

Production Editor: Doogri Institute

ISBN 978-1-7342079-1-0

Practice Assignments

🦖 Practice everything once.
🦖 Skip a day between practice.
🦖 Practice three times each week.

DATE | PIECES | NOTES | ✓ ✓ ✓

Contents

401. Middle C
402. Dini's Song
403. Who Is First?
404. Sky Song
405. Mister Treble
406. Scooba Chase
407. Green Balloon
408. Humorous
409. Sight Sing
410. Whole Notes
411. Heart Song
412. Popcorn Barn
413. Funny Dreams
414. Rainbow
415. Jonah From Arizona
416. Who's There?
417. Creature Twins
418. Mama Bee
419. Expectations
420. Look for Me
421. Owl Song
422. Beauty Queens
423. Cattle Jam
424. Play and Rest
425. Double Time
426. Hamster Wheel
427. Midnight Lights
428. Ensembles
429. Fourths In My Mind
430. Precious Be
431. Headlights
432. Shalom Shabbat
433. Time For Change
434. Al and Etta
435. Grandpa G
436. Zeidy's Boy
437. Solfege Hunting
438. Gondola
439. Shake It Up
440. Blue Notes
441. Lullaby
442. Lullaby in C
443. Snackers

401. Middle C

🦖 "Mommy Hand" (RH) plays the middle C.

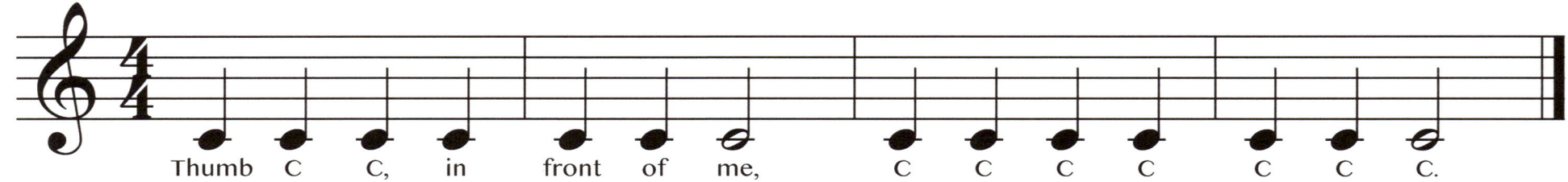

Thumb C C, in front of me, C C C C C C C.

402. Dini's Song

🦖 Play all the D notes.

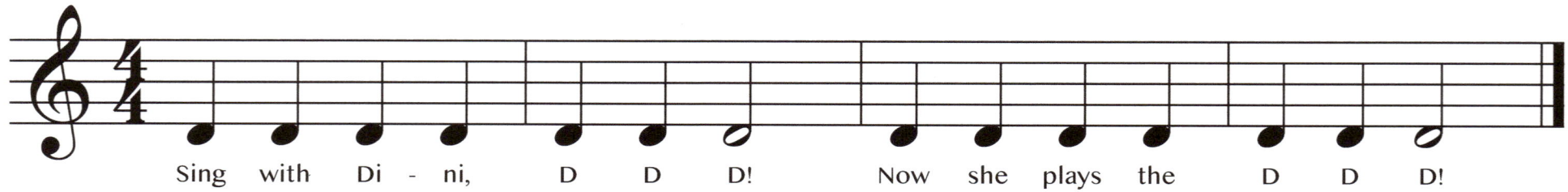

Sing with Di - ni, D D D! Now she plays the D D D!

403. Who Is First?

🦖 Imagine the sound of your five fingers.
🦖 Who is first—C or D?

Find it, play it. Learn to count. Steps move 'round to build a sound

High and dear the C I hear, same notes can be nice and clear.

404. Sky Song

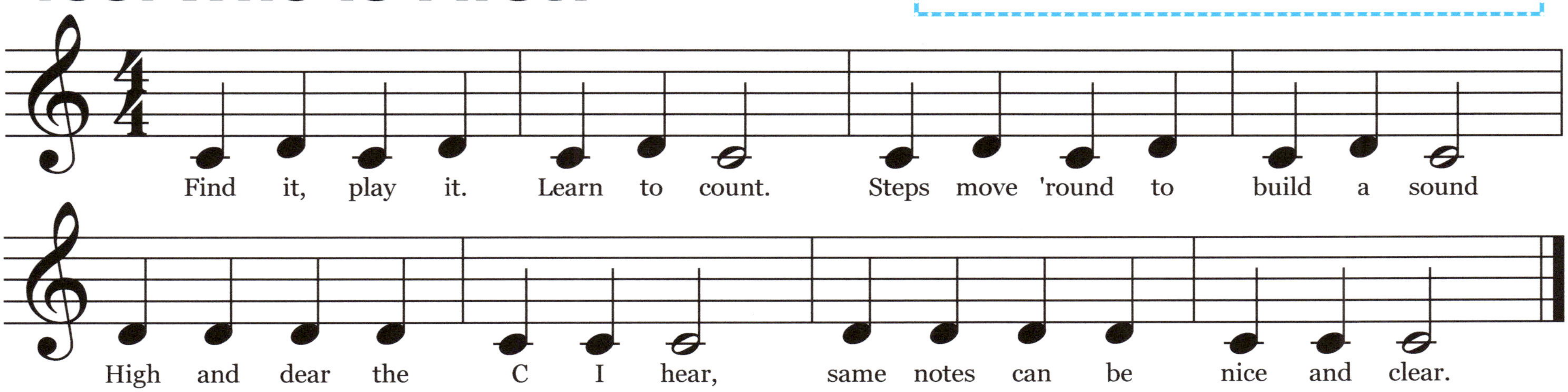

🦖 Sing the steps and guess the notes.

Wea-ther changed, col-der days, birds don't want to stay and play.

Blue sky has no clouds I see, birds flew south so they won't freeze.

405. Mister Treble

> 🦖 Play all the notes on the G-line.

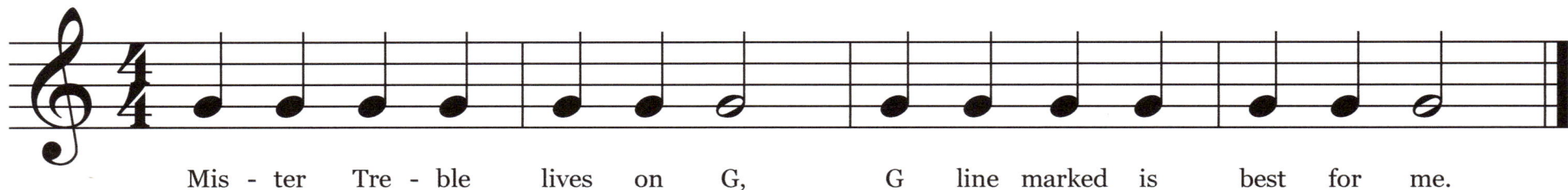

Mis - ter Tre - ble lives on G,   G line marked is best for me.

🦖 Mark the G-line by stretching it away from the Treble Clef.

🦖 Why do you think it used to be called "the G Clef"?

406. Scooba Chase

🦖 Mark the G-line for the whole song.

🦖 G-line or one under?

🦖 Play the repeat sign again for the 2nd verse of lyrics.

4 counts   **play-hold-hold-hold**

Saw a snail go chase a whale a - round the wa - ter pail. Scoo - ba doo - ba day.
Saw a whale then chase the snail a - round his shi - ny tail. Doo - ba scoo - ba yay.

406-A. Add More Verses

🦖 Write another verse, then sing it to this tune. Does it rhyme?

Saw a_____, _____ chase _____

Scooba, dooba, day!

Saw a_____, _____ chase _____

Scooba, dooba, yay!

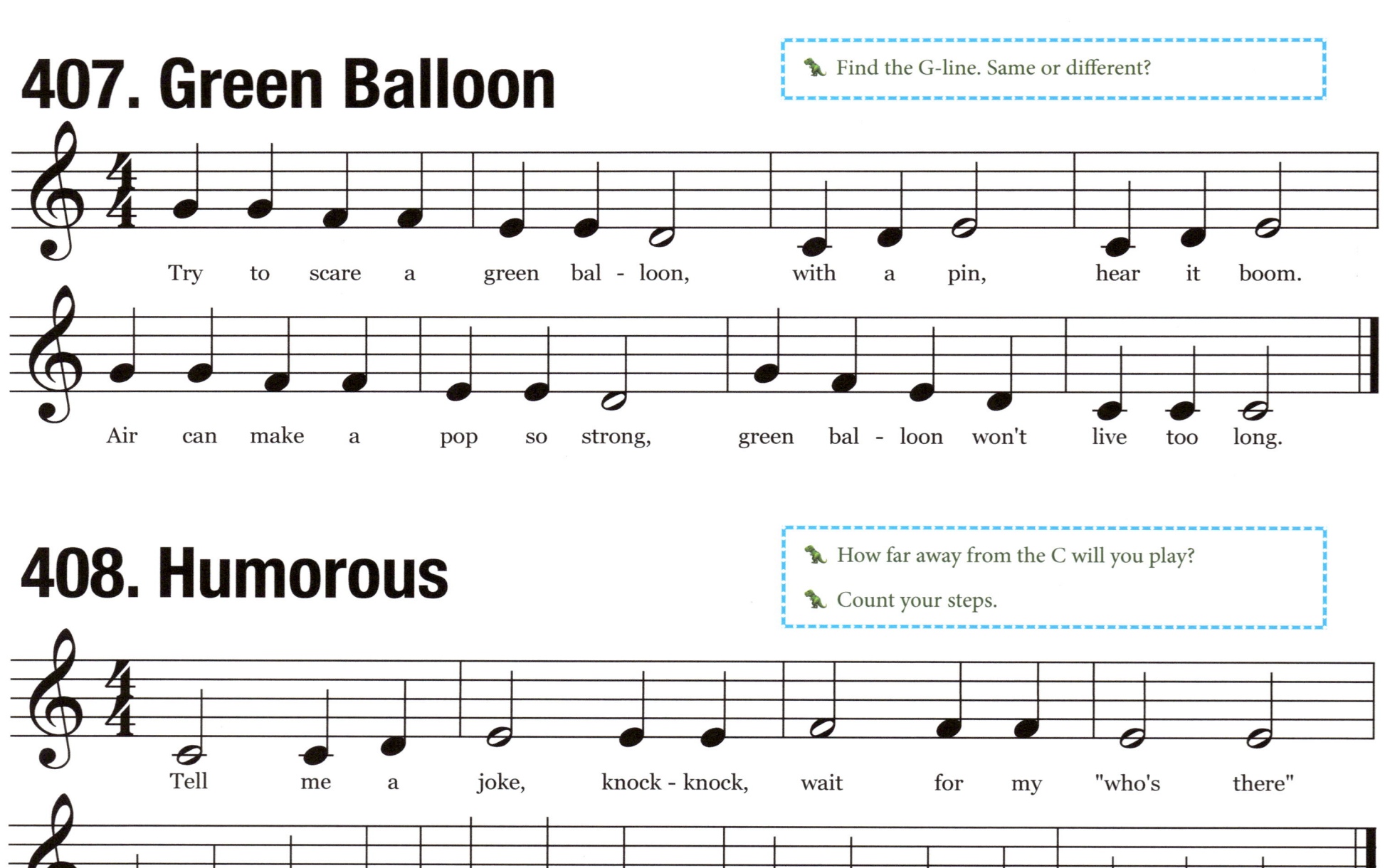

409. Sight Sing

🦖 Sing the letter names BEFORE you play.
🦖 Can you hear it in your head?

 4/4 plays 4 beats per measure. Count 4 beats until the next |barline|.

410. Whole Notes

🦖 Whole notes have no stem.
🦖 Hold for 4 counts, "play-hold-hold-hold".

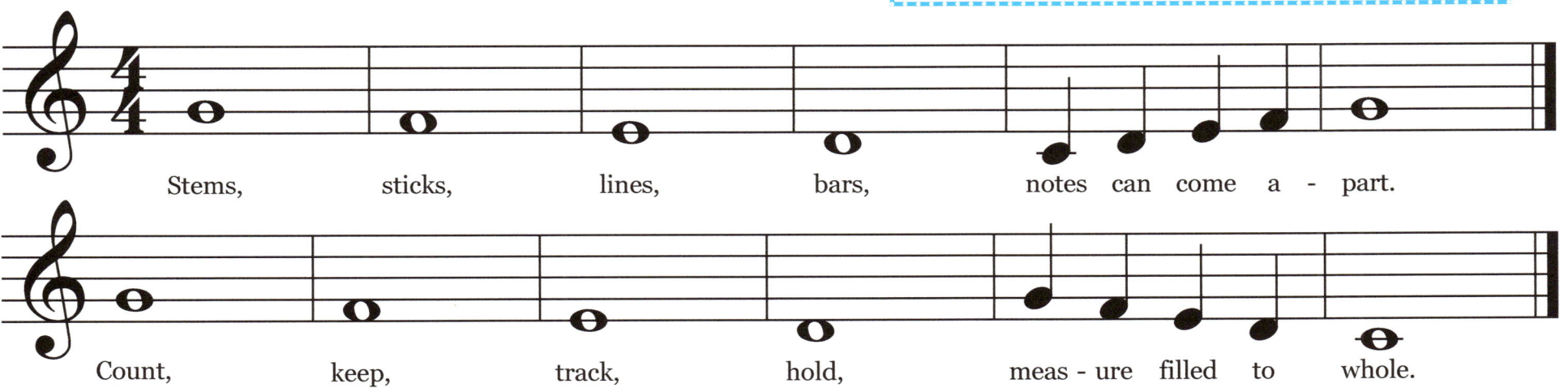

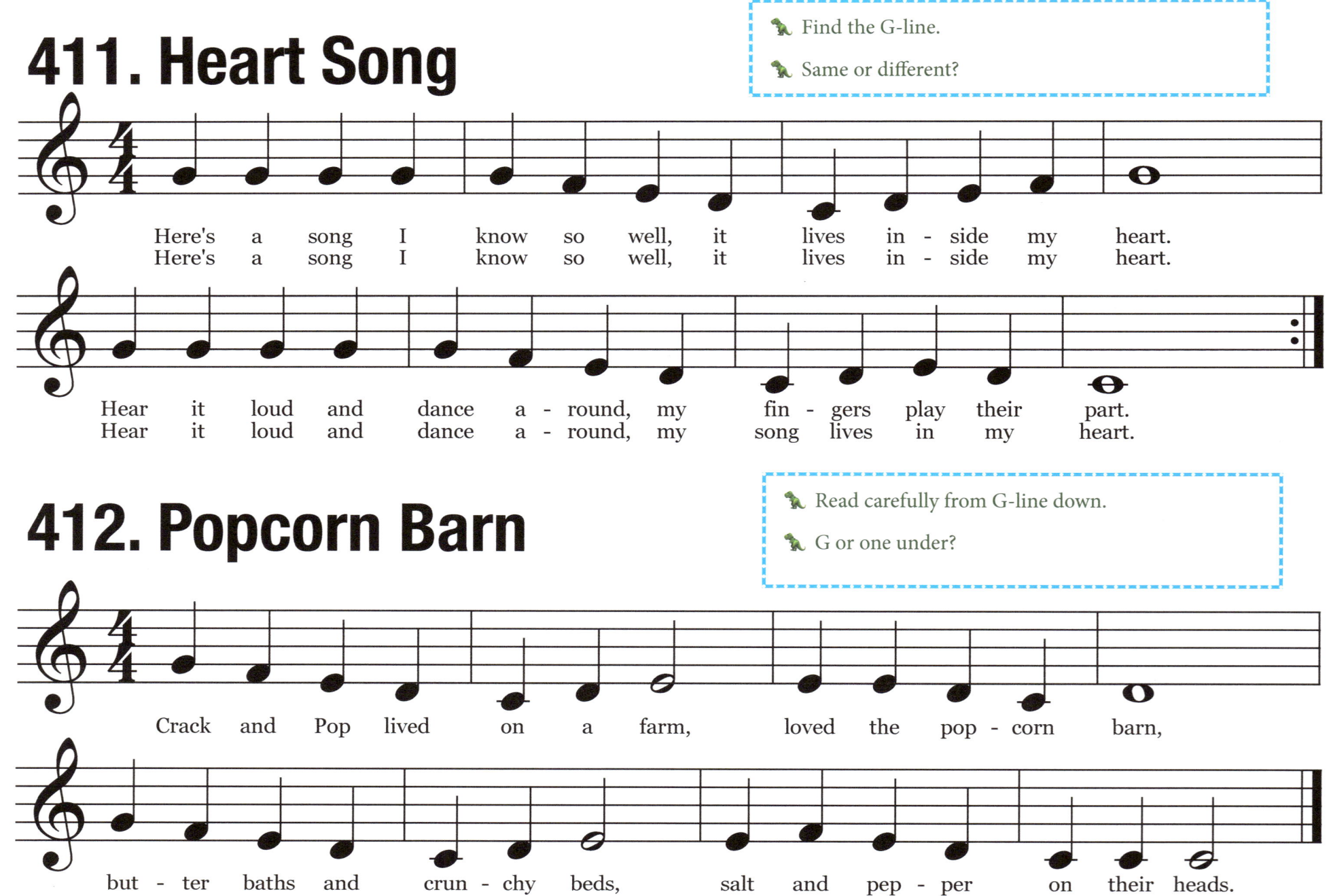

413. Funny Dreams

🦖 Play from the C and up.

🦖 Same or different? Count your steps.

 Play a second up or down. A melodic 2nd is always 1-up or 1-down.

Last night I had fun-ny dreams, ate some cake with tooth-paste cream.
Ma-ma asked if I want more, thank you, no! It made me snore.

413-A. Change The Lyrics

🦖 Write your dream, then sing your own lyrics to this tune. Does it rhyme?

Last night I had _____,

_____ some _____ with _____.

Mama asked if _____,

Thank you, _____ It _____.

414. Rainbow

🦖 Dotted-half note holds for 3 beats.

🦖 2nds-step-step.

🦖 Same notes tied together adds more beats to hold. Think: 3+3=?

💡 3/4 plays 3 beats per measure. Count 3 beats until the next |barline|.

Play/hold/hold.   Tied/hold/hold   hold/hold/hold.

Rain - drops can shine bright as rays of light,

glow like an art - ist who cried

Mir - ror re - flec - tion from sun, up high.

Arc shapes of paint in the sky

415. Jonah from Arizona

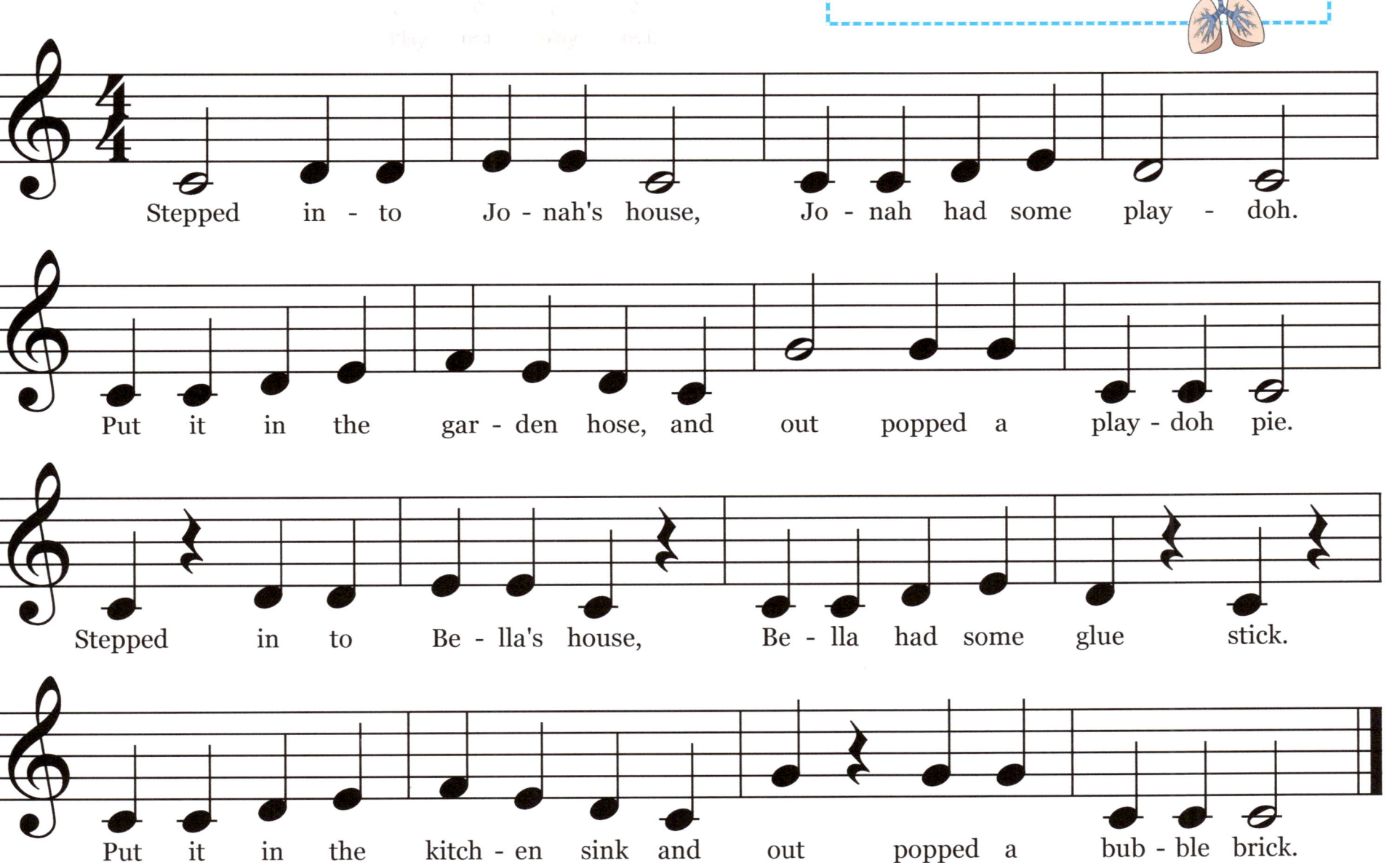

416. Who's There?

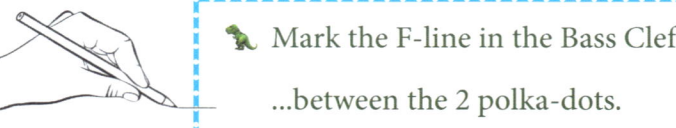

417. Creature Twins

418. Mama Bee

- Mark the Treble Clef G-line and Bass Clef F-line.
- Find the brace on the Grand Staff
- Find the position for both hands on the piano and play simultaneously.

 Who is holding, and who is walking?

Bring-ing home a bum-ble bee, Mom will be so proud of me,

Got a sting on my good side, Winked-an eye, and said good-bye.

Play melodic 2nds and 3rds.

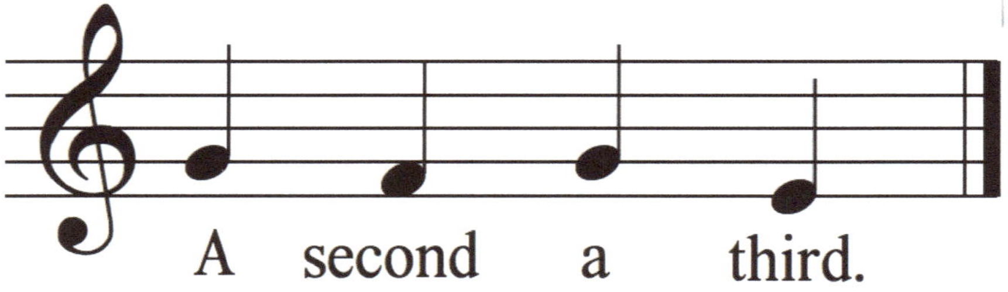
A second a third.

Play harmonic 2nds and 3rds.

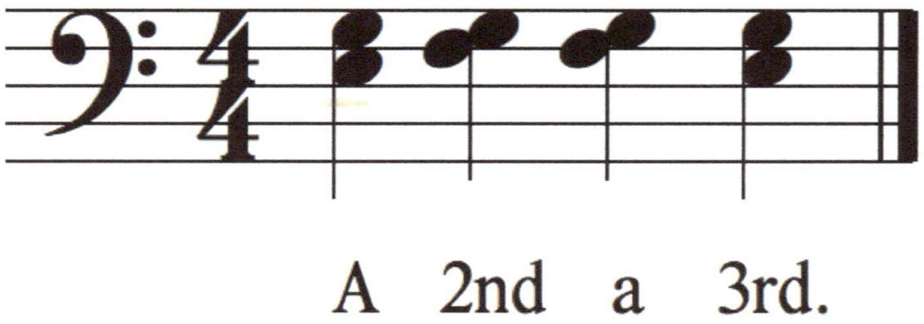
A 2nd a 3rd.

419. Expectations

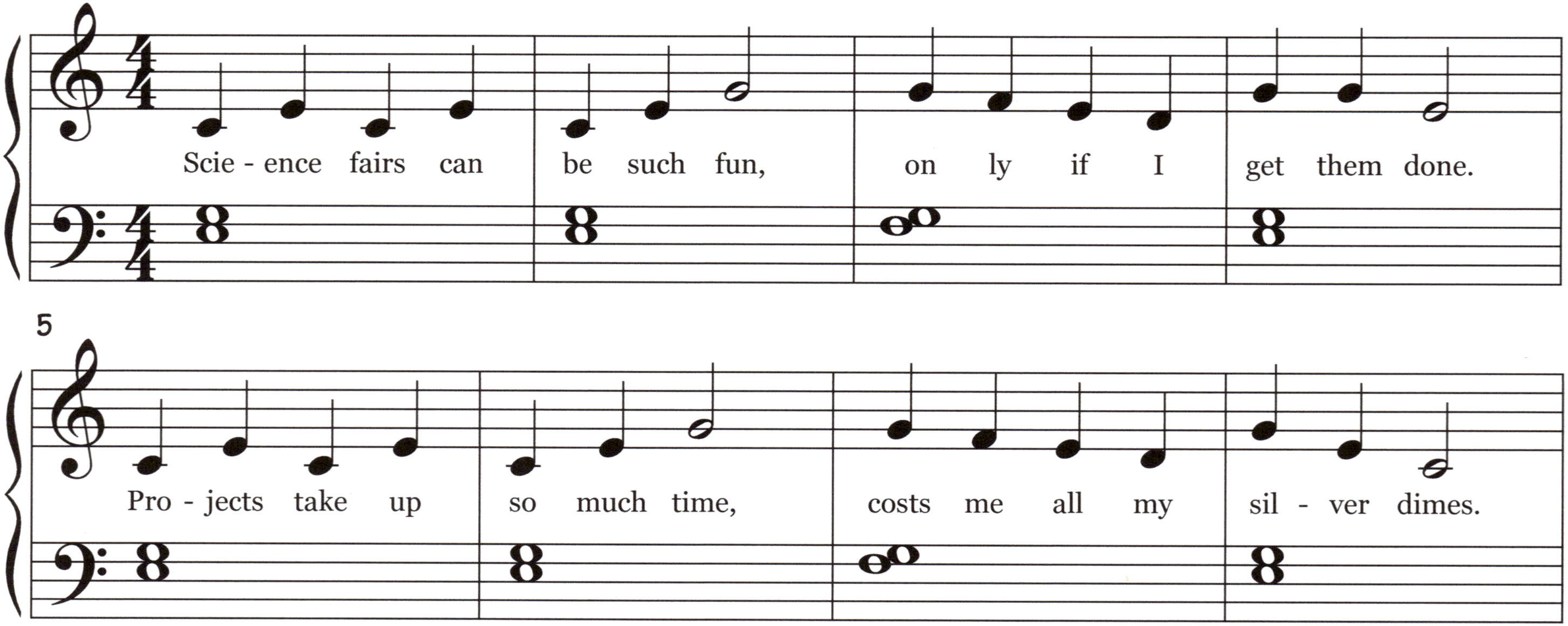
Scie - ence fairs can be such fun, on ly if I get them done.
5
Pro - jects take up so much time, costs me all my sil - ver dimes.

There are 1,500 active volcanoes in the world, with nearly 200 in the United States.

Yellowstone National Park is actually the caldera of a supervolcano.

Recently, the Hawaiian Big Island was home to an entire lake of lava.

420. Look For Me

> 🦖 Mark the Treble Clef G-line and Bass Clef F-line.
> 🦖 Count the steps from each note.

 Play melodic 2nds from line-to-space or space-to-line.
Play melodic 3rds from line-to-line or space-to-space.

🦖 Who plays first? Treble or Bass?

A second a third.

421. Owl Song

🦖 Play 3rds from line-to-line or space-to-space.

🦖 Same or different?

🦖 3/4 plays 3 beats per measure. Count 3 beats until the next |barline|.

Play/hold/hold.

💡 **Play harmonic 2nds and 3rds.**

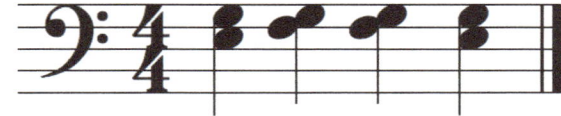

A 2nd a 3rd.

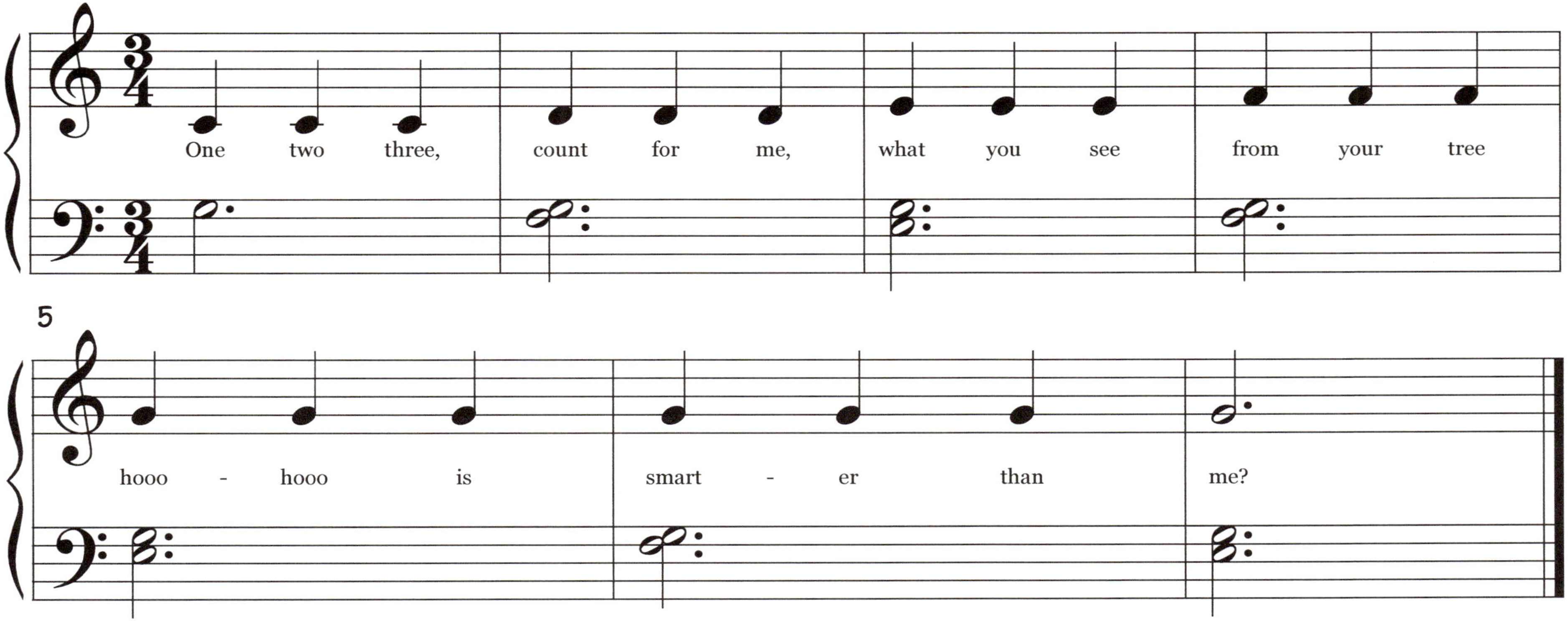

One two three, count for me, what you see from your tree

hooo - hooo is smart - er than me?

422. Beauty Queens

- Conduct nose to belly button.
- Palm is facing the floor.

Conducting in 4/4 time while singing or playing

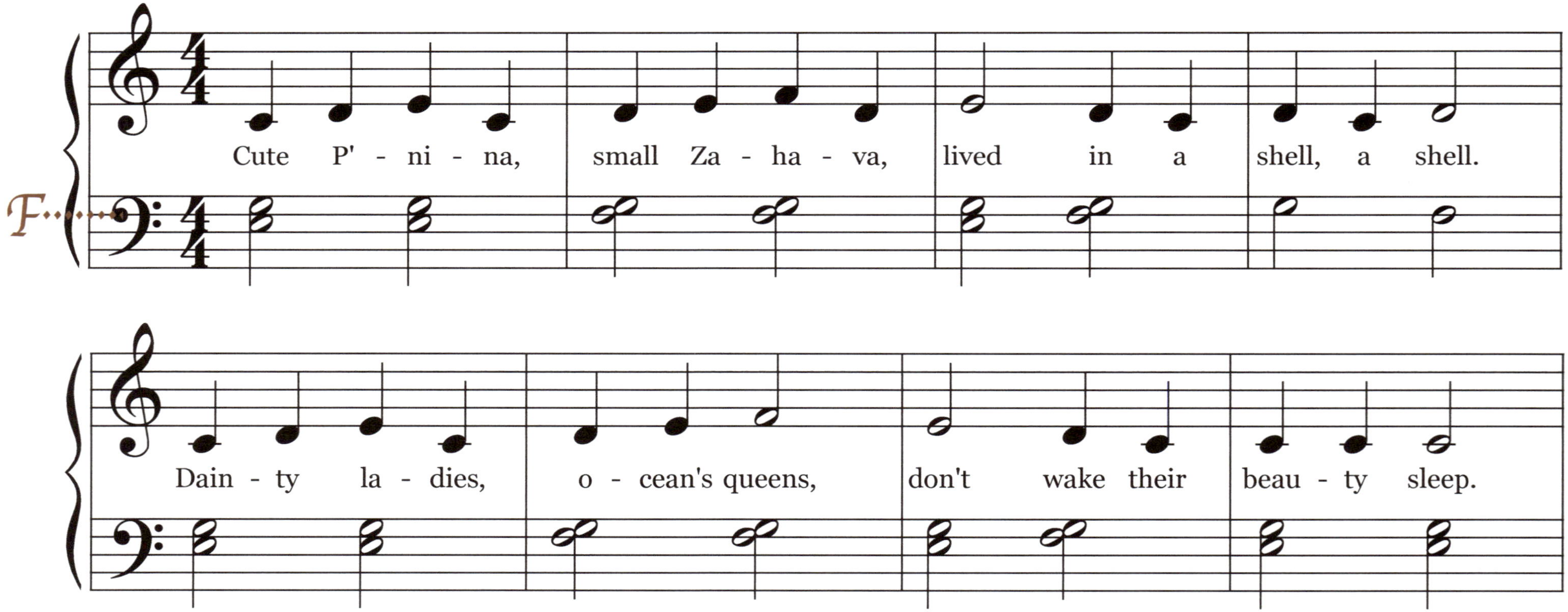

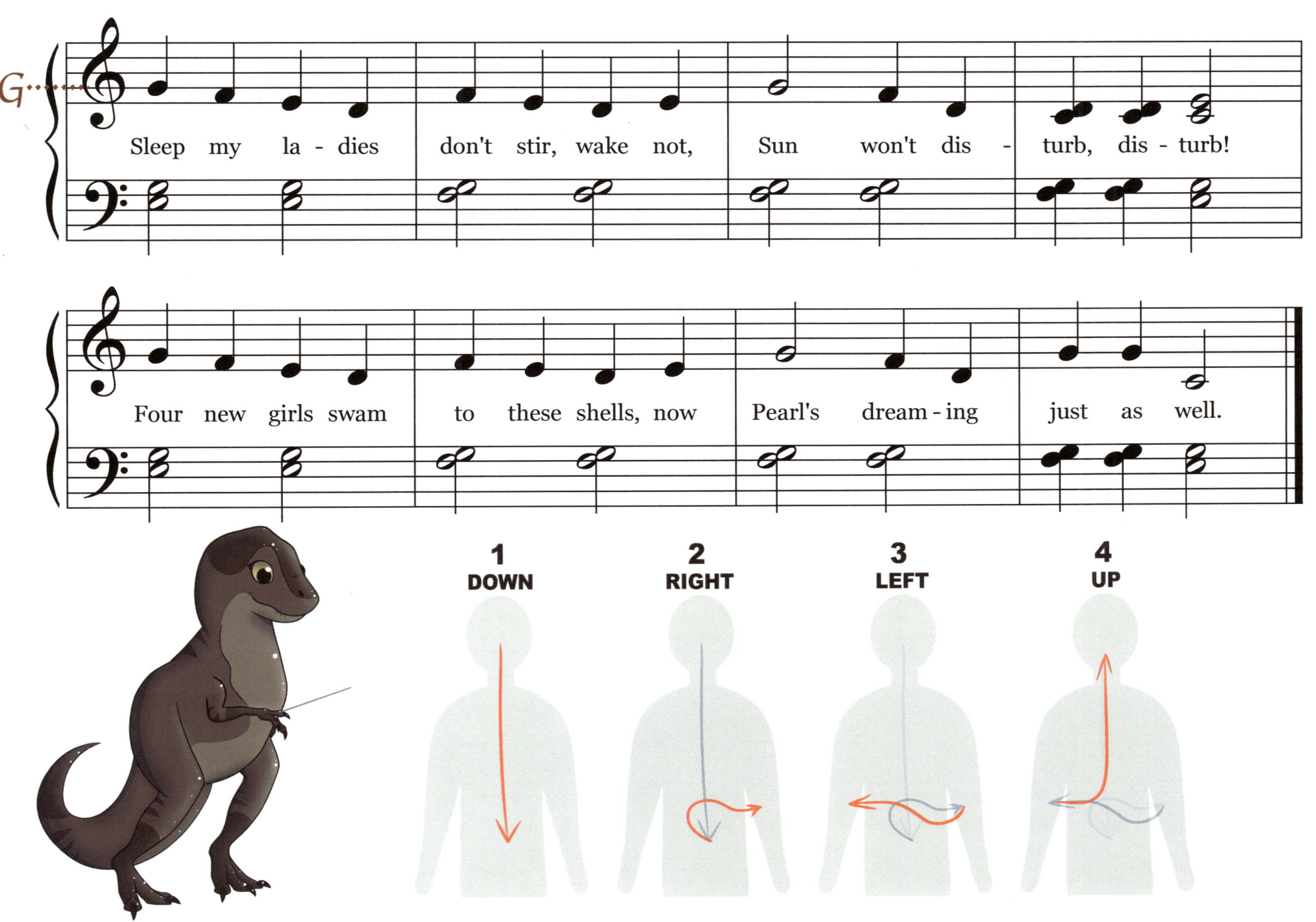

423. Cattle Jam

 G-line or 1-under?

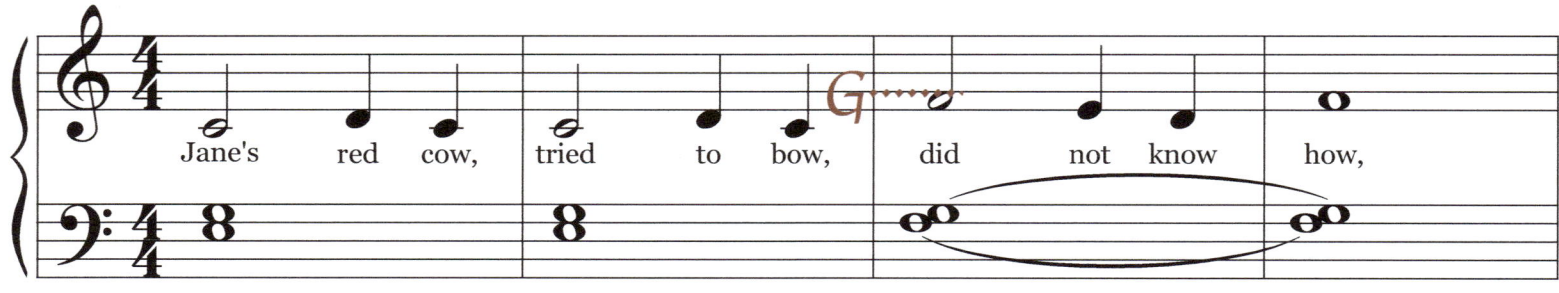

Whole notes tied holds for 4+4

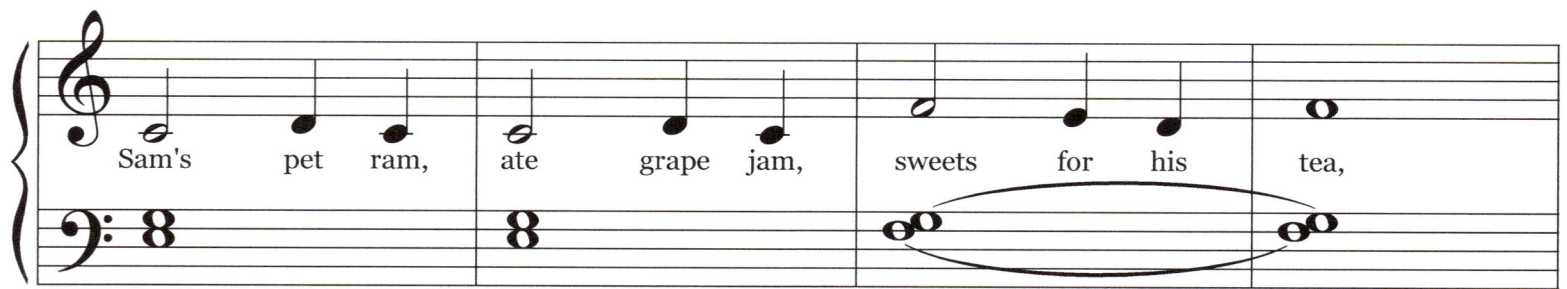

424. Play and Rest

> 🦖 Play 3rds from line-to-line or space-to-space.
> 🦖 Same or different?
> 🦖 Hold the harmonic 2nds and 3rds in Bass Clef

💡 Each rest sign is silent for 1 beat.

💡 **Play harmonic 2nds or 3rds.**

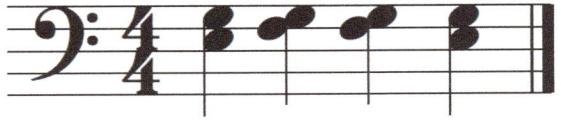

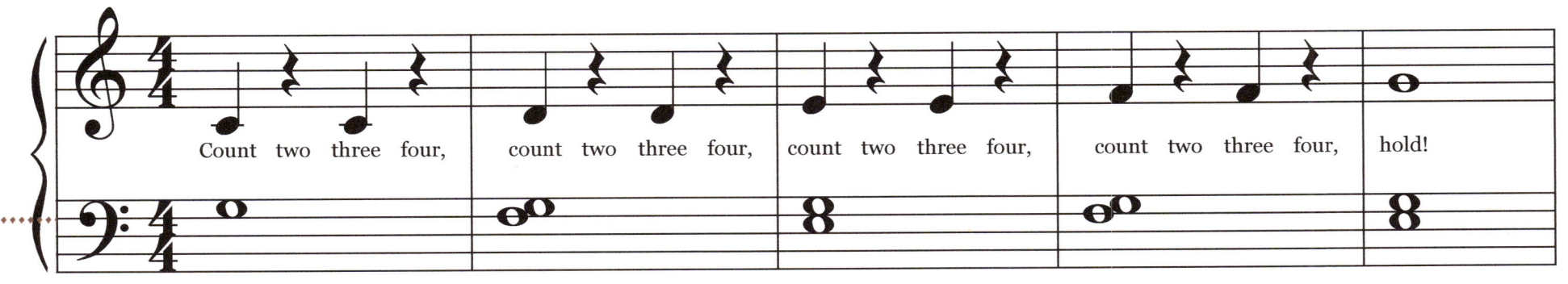

425. Double Time

> 🦖 The "P" piano sign is for soft playing.
> 🦖 Play accent signs louder than the "P" volume.
> 🦖 Play slurs in Legato smooth style.

 **Slurs connect different notes inside a musical phrase.**

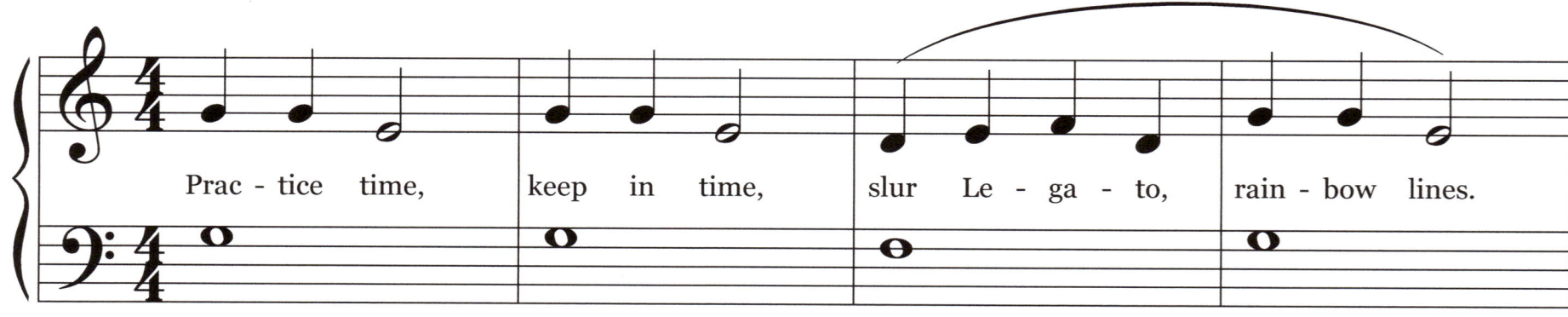

Prac - tice time, keep in time, slur Le - ga - to, rain - bow lines.

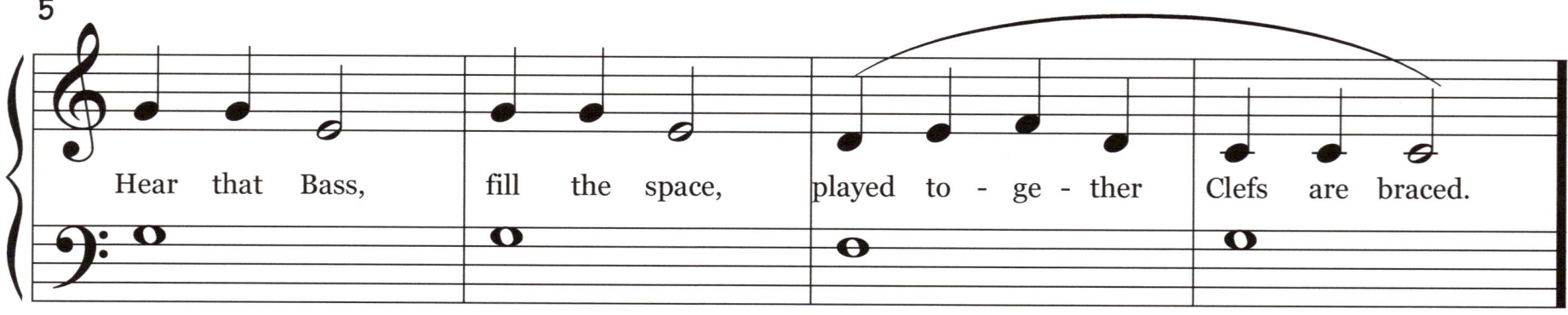

Hear that Bass, fill the space, played to - ge - ther Clefs are braced.

9

Prac - tice time, Tre - ble rhymes, hands to - ge - ther all the time.

13

> > > >
Ac - cent sign, loud this time, slur Le - ga - to rain - bow lines.

 **Names with accents.**

> > > >
Henry   Henry   Penny   Penny

426. Hamster Wheel

427. Midnight Lights

G-line down a 3rd to?

428. Ensembles

Conduct nose to belly button.

Palm is facing the floor.

Conducting in 3/4 time while singing or playing

5
flutes, - and horns, and trum - pets,
make up the brass in en - sem - bles.

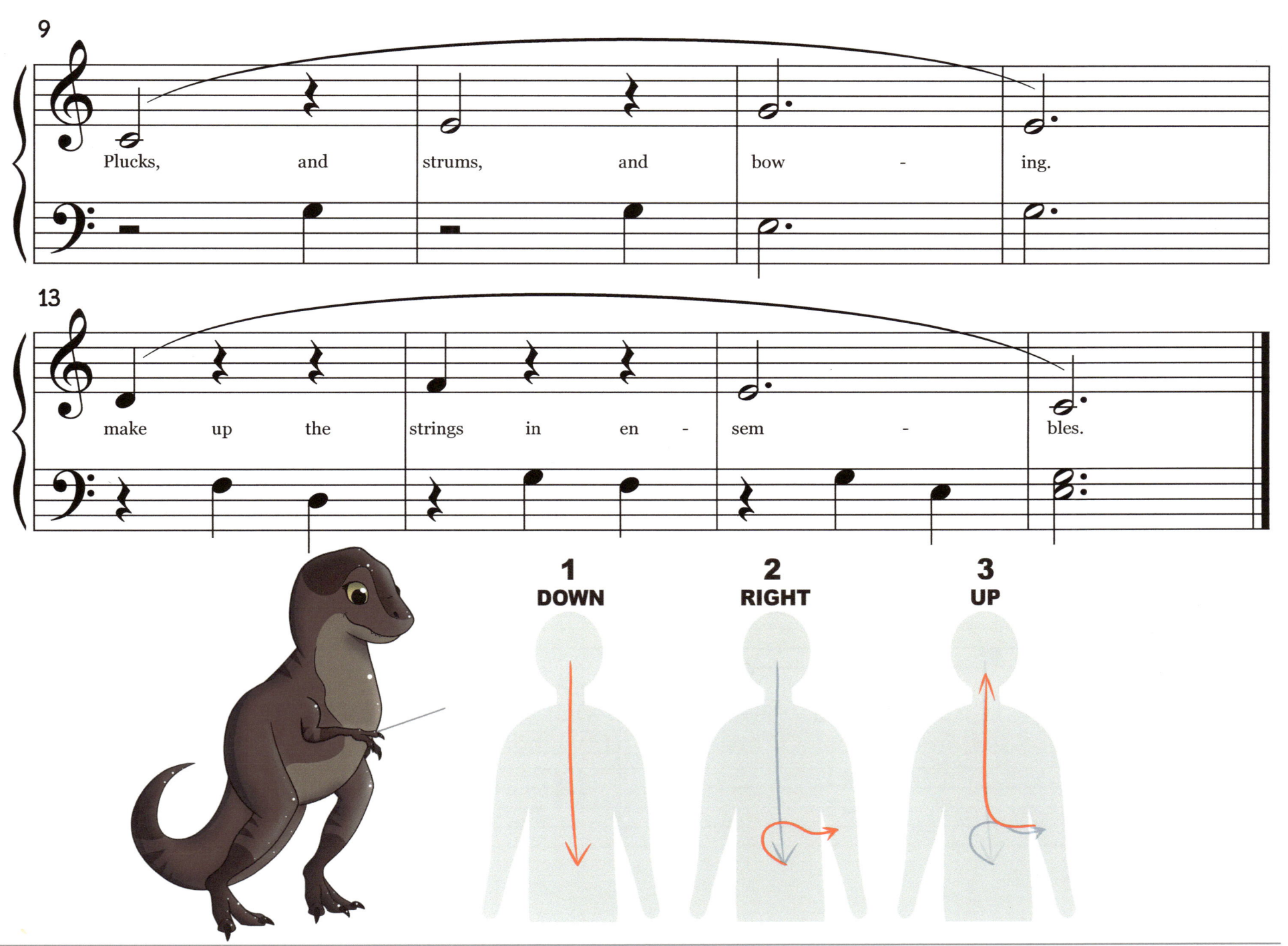

429. Fourths In My Mind

 **Play melodic 4ths from line-to-space or space-to-line.
Find the harmonic 4ths in the Bass Clef.**

Thoughts in my mind, hear me, what do you think.
Quick don't think more, I don't need one more thought.

Thoughts in my mind, hear me, what do you think.
Quick ask me what are my thoughts that I feel.

430. Precious Be

Moderato

> 🦖 How far away from the F-line will you start?
> 🦖 Speed up your reading. Trust your mirror-fingers.

Look in the mir - ror and what do you see, I see me on - ly me it's the best me I can be. I am so pre - cious, I'm glad to be me, I see shapes and hear sounds, I see me, all a - round.

MODERATO: Italian for moderate or medium walking speed.

431. Headlights

- An incomplete measure is called a pickup beat or anacrusis.
- The anacrusis is always completed in the last measure.

4 1 2 3 4 1 2 3

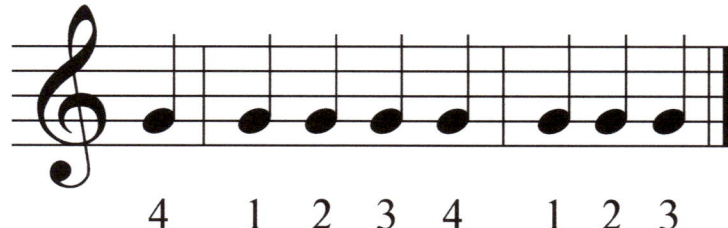

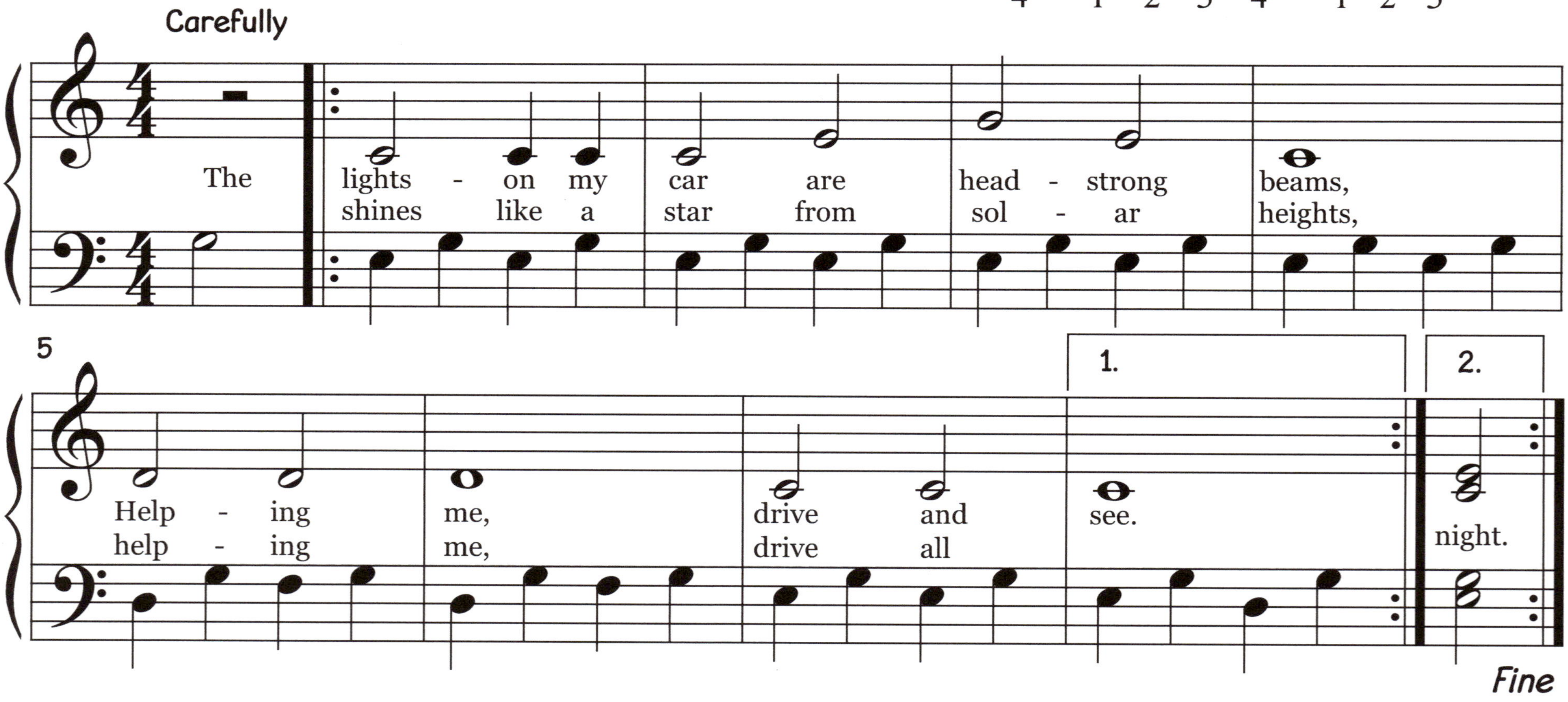
Carefully
The
lights - on my car are head - strong beams,
shines like a star from sol - ar heights,
5
1.
2.
Help - ing me, drive and see.
help - ing me, drive all
night.
Fine

Conduct a preparatory gesture for the incomplete measure. Count how many incomplete beats you must conduct before the first complete measure.

432. Shalom Shabbat

The glue on Israeli stamps is Kosher.

There are more Jewish people living in New York City than in all of Israel!

In 1952, Albert Einstein was asked to be the president of Isreal, but he declined.

% of Israeli homes use solar energy to heat water!

The smallest subway system in the world is in Haifa, Israel. It contains only four carriages and a 1.8 km. track.

f Bim bam bim bam, bim bim bim bam, Fri-day-night, Shab-bat-time.

p Can-dle-light-ing house is shin-ing, Mind set for res-ting time.

Shab-bat, Sha-lom, bim, bam. Shab-bat, Sha-lom bim, bam!

f Bim bam bim bam, bim bim bim bam, Frid-day night, Shab-bat time.

433. Time For Change

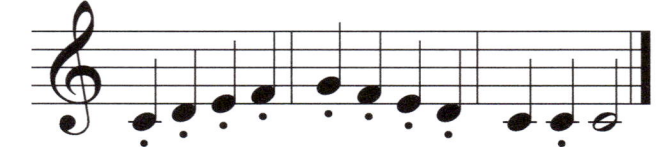
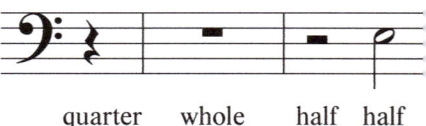

quarter whole half half

STACCATO
Italian for detatched.

Staccato is notated with a dot above or below the notehead.

PUSHKA:
Hebrew for a charity box.

MITZVAH:
Hebrew for a good deed.

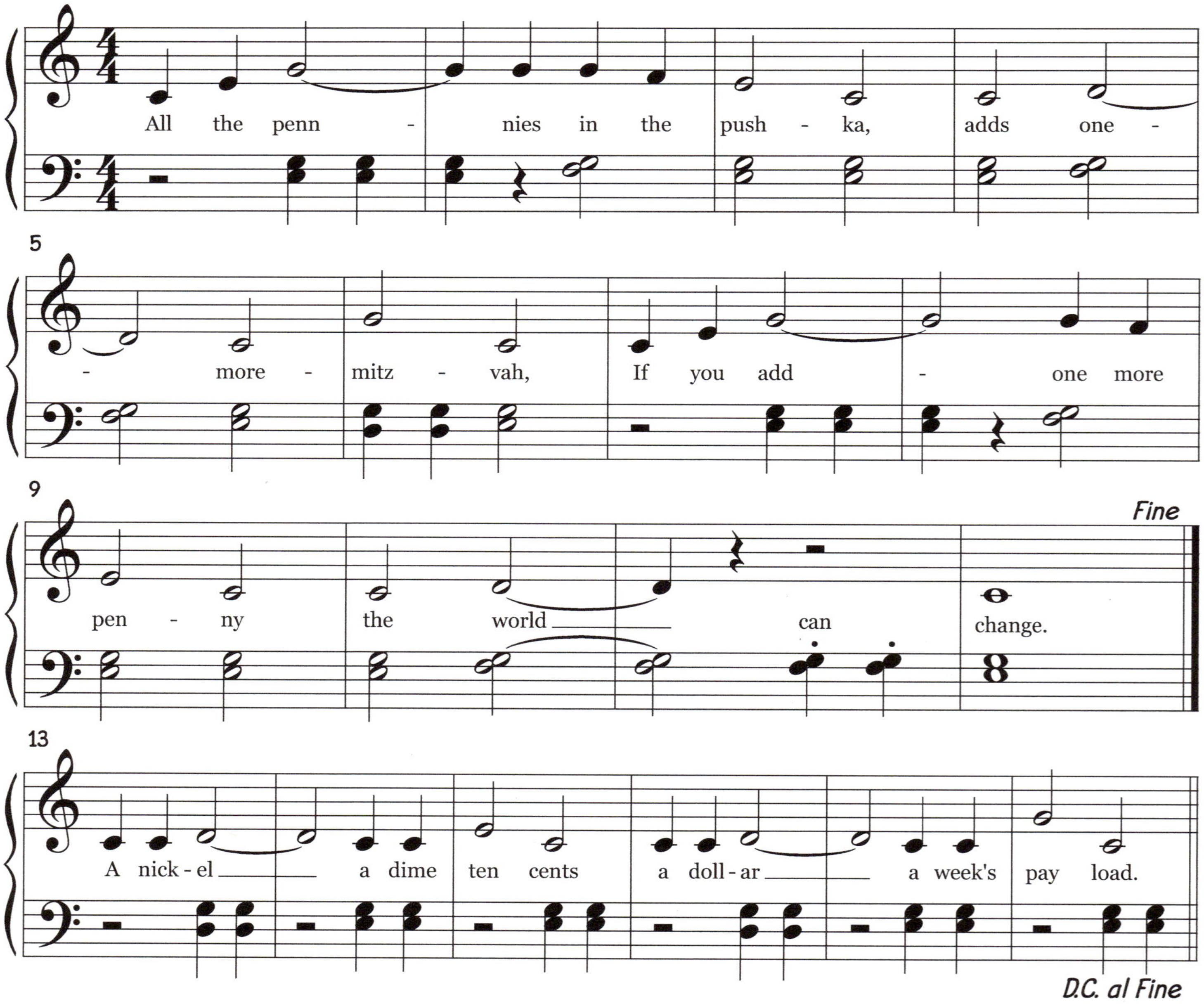

All the penn - nies in the push - ka, adds one -

more mitz - vah, If you add one more

pen - ny the world can change.

Fine

A nick - el a dime ten cents a doll - ar a week's pay load.

D.C. al Fine

434. Al and Etta

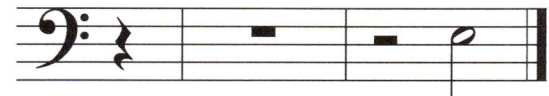
quarter whole half half

D.C. al Fine:
Italian for
Da Capo al Fine.

Play until the D.C. and then return to the beginning to play until the Fine, which is the final ending of the piece.

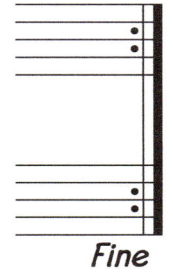

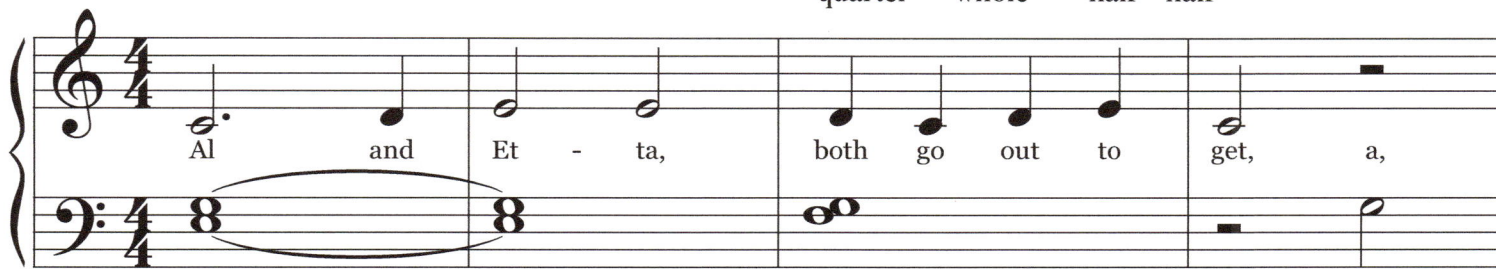
Al and Et - ta, both go out to get, a,

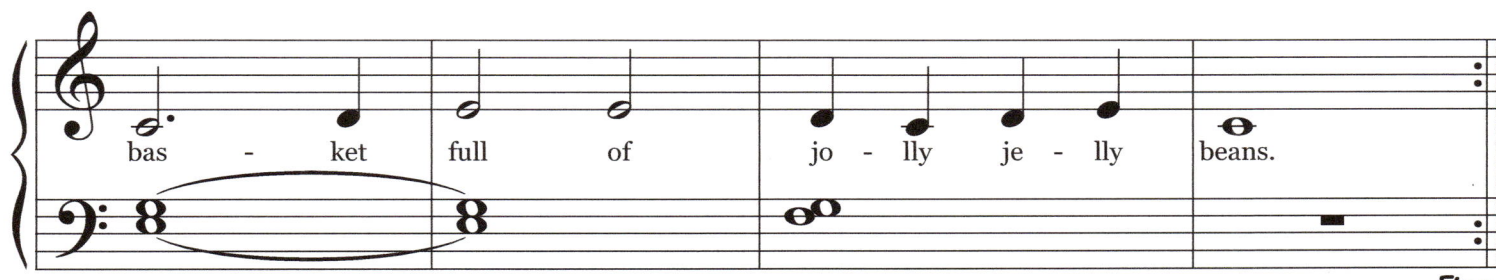
bas - ket full of jo - lly je - lly beans. *Fine*

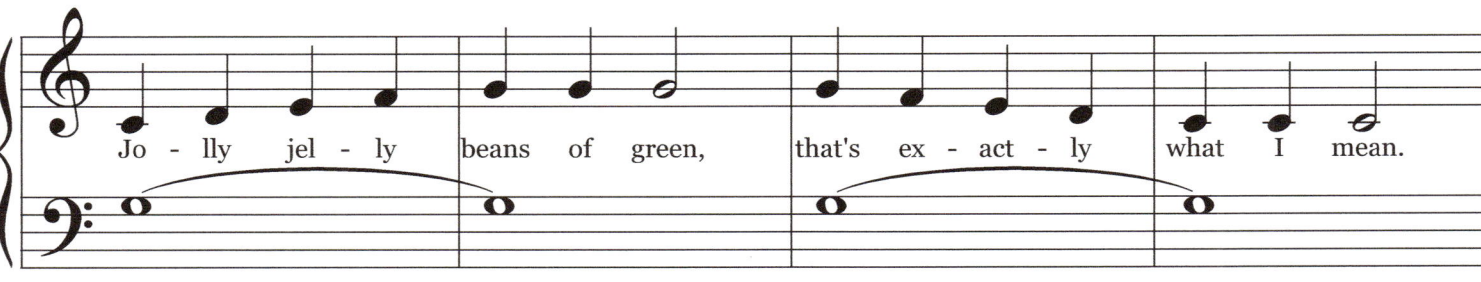
Jo - lly jel - ly beans of green, that's ex - act - ly what I mean.

Beans so green! Beans so green! oh, oh, oh, oh! *D.C. al Fine*

435. Grandpa G

> 🦖 Put both hands in G position.

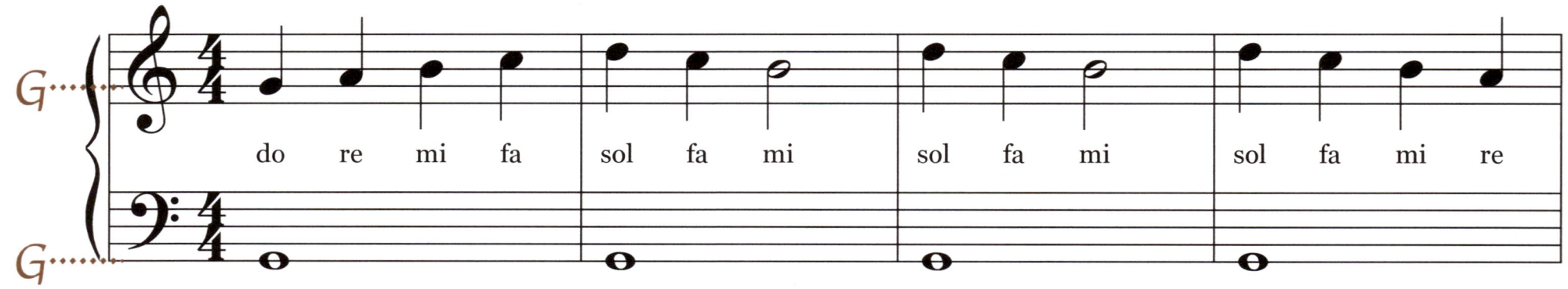

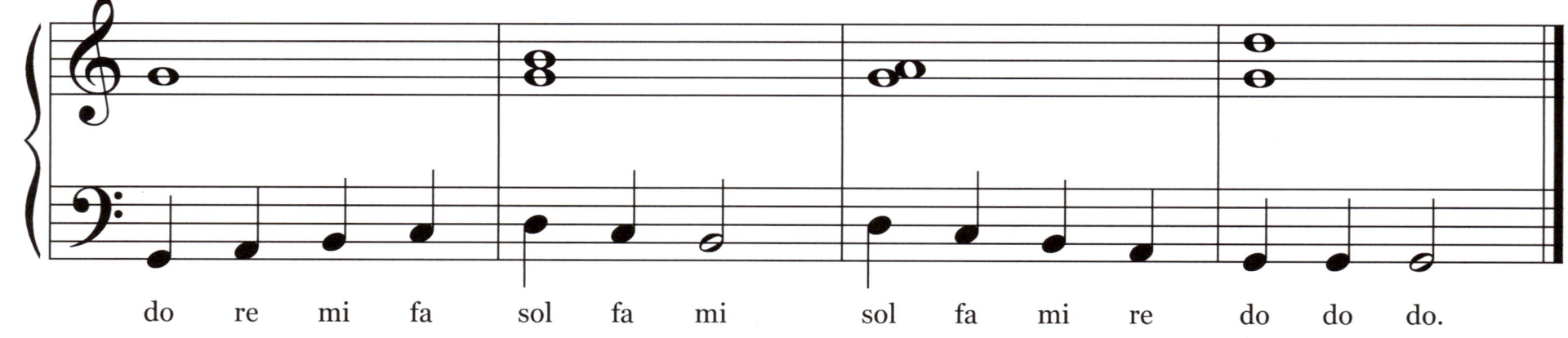

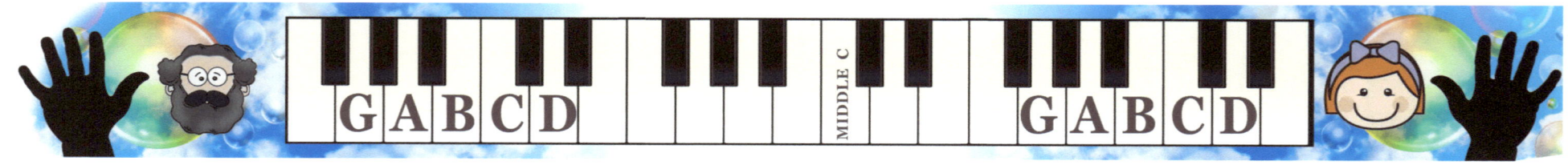

436. Zeidy's Boy

🦖 How far away from Grandpa G-line will you play in the Bass Clef?
🦖 Count the melodic intervals to figure out the solfege.

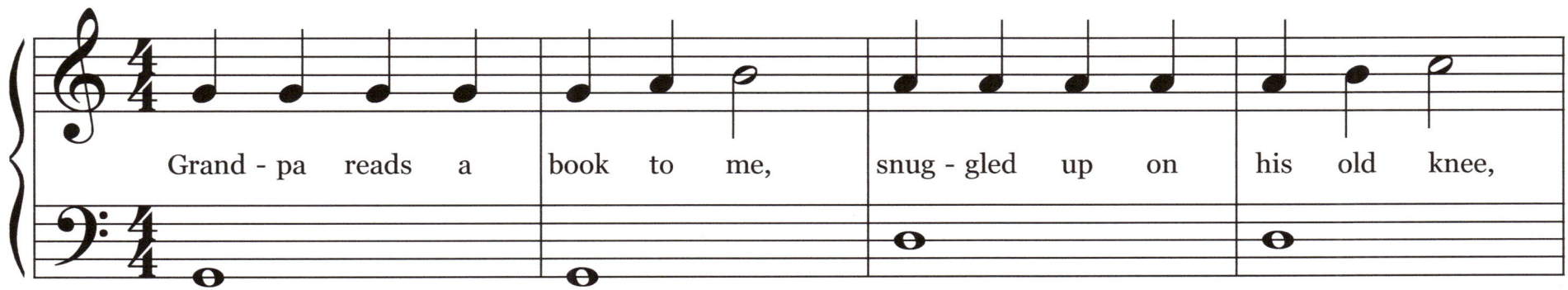

Grand-pa reads a book to me, snug-gled up on his old knee,

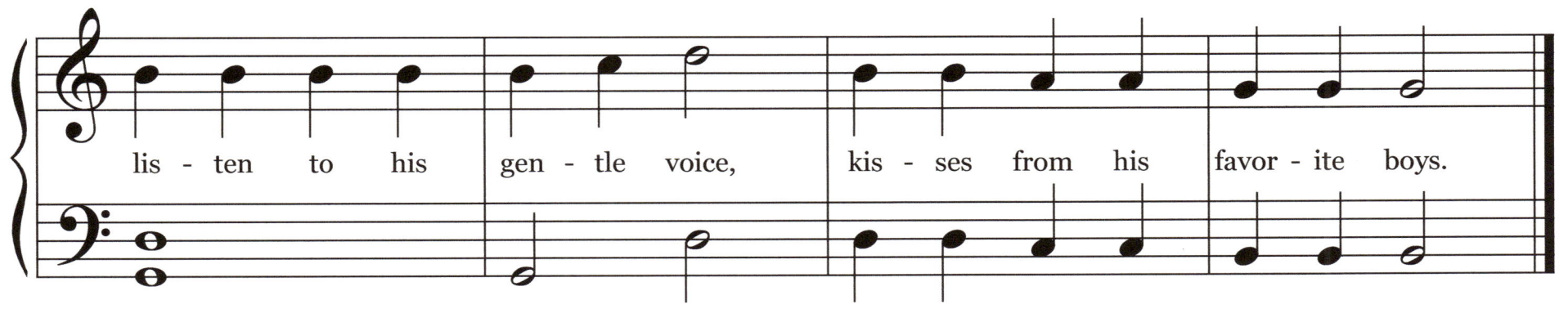

lis-ten to his gen-tle voice, kis-ses from his favor-ite boys.

Solfège

French for a universal language for musical notes so that people from all around the world can make music together.

                         sol
                fa   fa
        mi   mi
    re   re
do   do

437. Solfège Hunting

🦖 Don't forget to mark all of the G-lines.

438. Gondola

439. Shake It Up

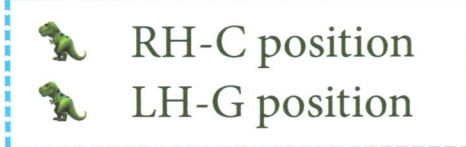
RH-C position
LH-G position

RITARDANDO:
Italian for slowly slowing down.

FERMATA:
Hold the note with a fermata as long as you want.

A TEMPO:
Resume your original speed (adante).

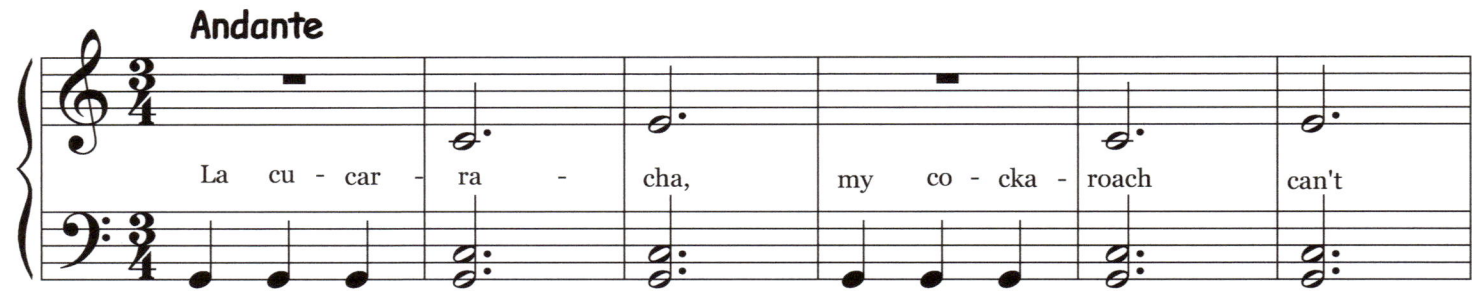

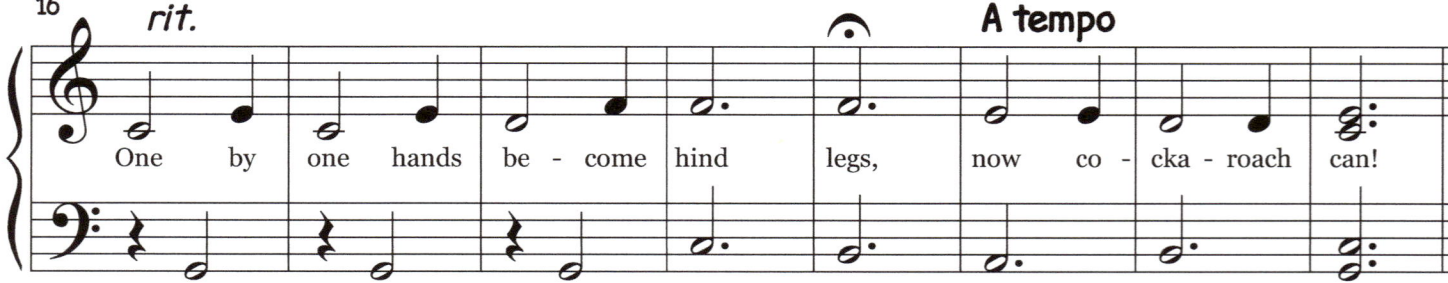

Conduct in 3/4 time.
Stretch your gesture to hold the fermata.
Conduct a cutoff when you want the fermata to end.

440. Blue Notes

🦖 A flat before a note modifies the solfege and is played 1 step to the left.

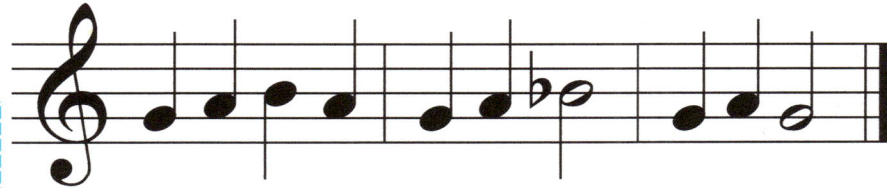

Some-times I try, hold back my cries, dark - ness, black - filled blue times.

Some - times I try, think - ing of light, change is in my life.

440-A. Blue Notes Again

🦖 Here is the same piece in C position.

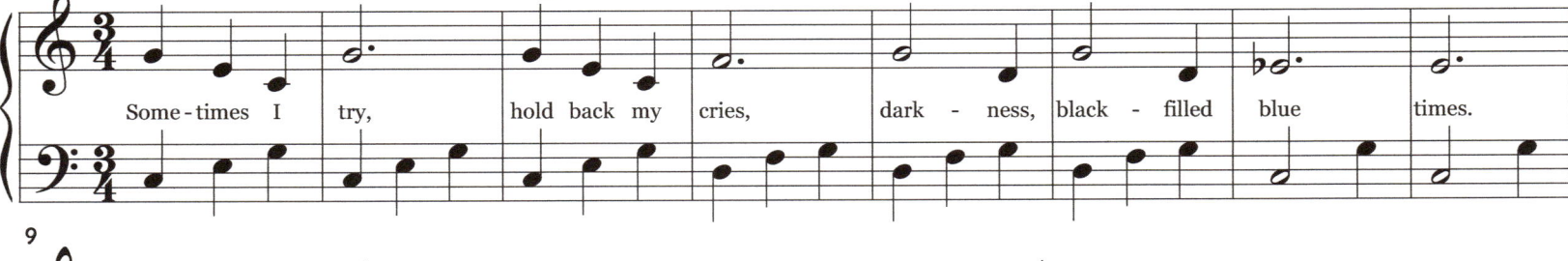

Some-times I try, hold back my cries, dark - ness, black - filled blue times.

TRANSPOSE:
Transpose to transfer any piece from one position to another. Use movable-Do to find the new starting point for both hands.

Some - times I try, think - ing of light, change is in my life.

441. Lullaby

> 🦖 A sharp before a note modifies the solfege and is played 1 step to the right. The bar line cancels the rule of sharps and flats.

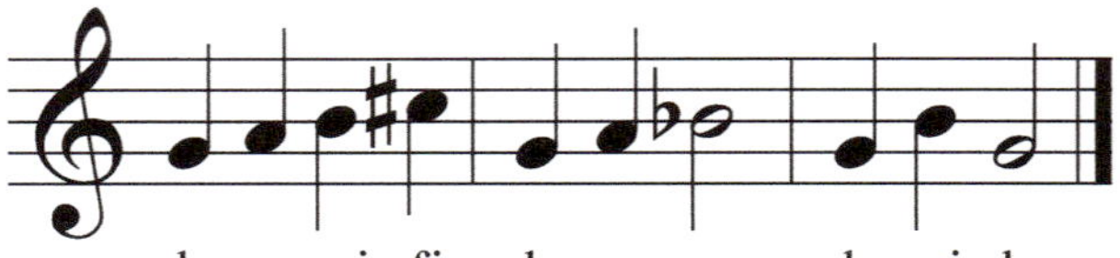

do re mi fi do re me, do mi do.

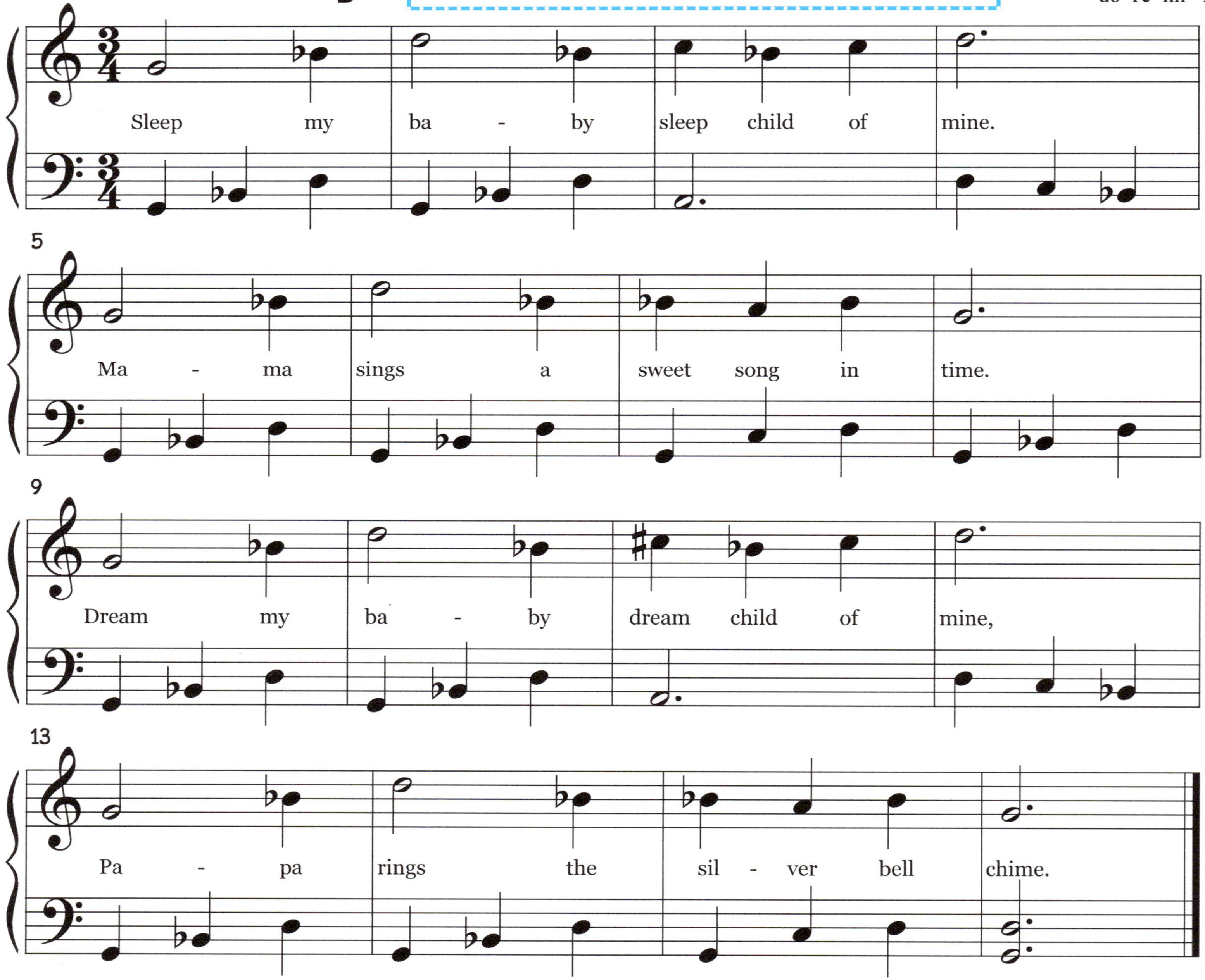

Sleep my ba - by sleep child of mine.

Ma - ma sings a sweet song in time.

Dream my ba - by dream child of mine,

Pa - pa rings the sil - ver bell chime.

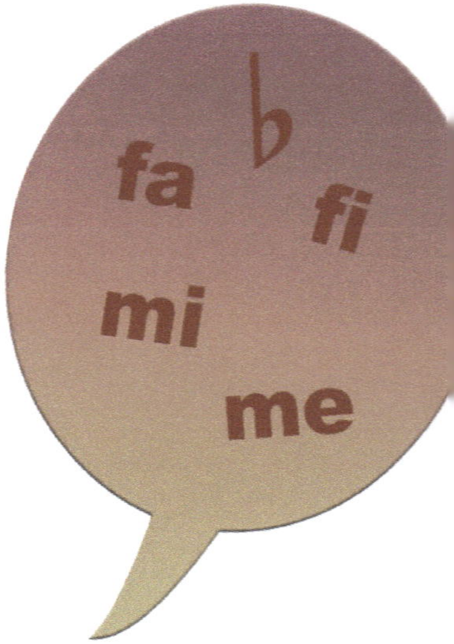

fa / fi
mi / me

Can you transpose to C?

442. Lullaby In C

TRANSPOSE:
Transpose to transfer any piece from one position to another. Use movable-Do to find the new starting point for both hands.

443. Snackers

> 🦖 An independent musician finds the Do.
> 🦖 Where will you place your hands on the piano? C or G position?

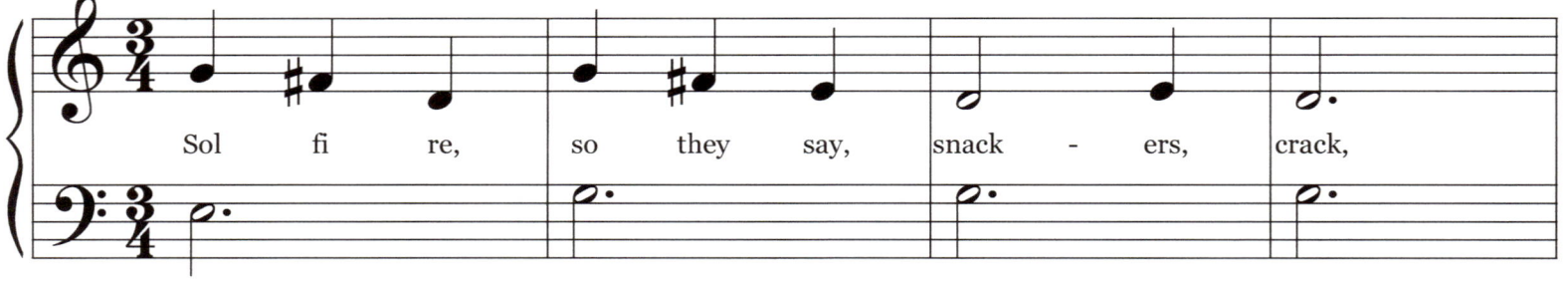
Sol fi re, so they say, snack-ers, crack,

Sol fi re, so they claim, crack-ers, pop!

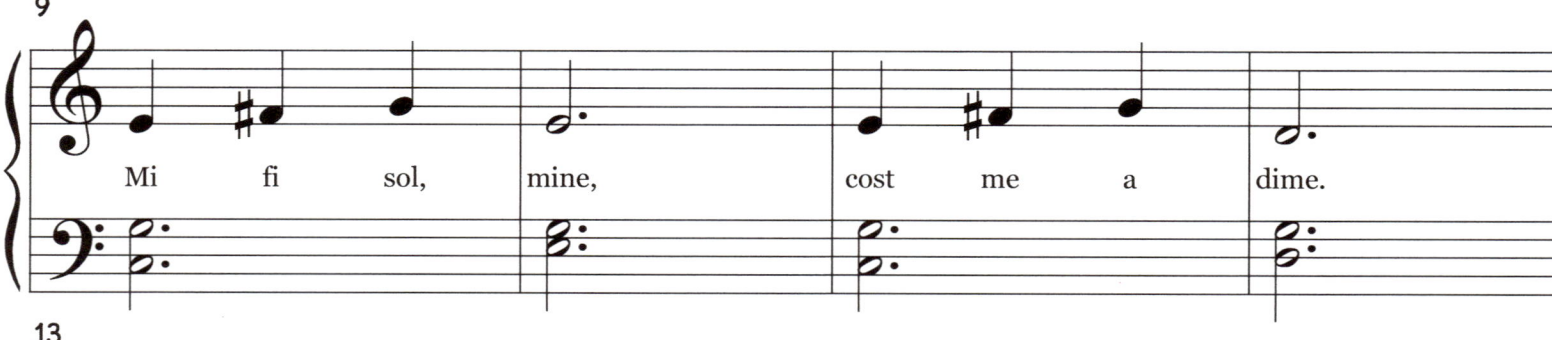
Mi fi sol, mine, cost me a dime.

Congratulations!

🦖 Book 2 is DONE!
🦖 Do you have Book 3 y
🦖 Look for the yellow co
    T-Rex will see you the

So feel my crack-ers, they crunch in this rhyme!

www.ingramcontent.com/pod-product-compliance
Lightning Source LLC
Chambersburg PA
CBHW041153070526

44584CB00004B/294